T0324252

# SOMETHING
## BLACK
#### IN THE
# GREEN PART
### OF YOUR EYE

# New Issues Poetry & Prose

| | |
|---|---|
| Editor | Herbert Scott |
| Associate Editor | David Dodd Lee |
| Advisory Editors | Nancy Eimers, Mark Halliday, William Olsen, J. Allyn Rosser |
| Assistants to the Editor | Rebecca Beech, Derek Pollard, Jonathan Pugh, Marianne E. Swierenga |
| Assistant Editors | Erik Lesniewski, Lydia Melvin, Adela Najarro, Margaret von Steinen |
| Editorial Assistants | Jennifer Abbott, Bethany Salgat |
| Business Manager | Michele McLaughlin |
| Fiscal Officer | Marilyn Rowe |

New Issues Poetry & Prose
The College of Arts and Sciences
Western Michigan University
Kalamazoo, MI 49008

*An Inland Seas Poetry Book*

 Inland Seas poetry books are supported by a grant from
The Michigan Council for Arts and Cultural Affairs.

First Edition, 2002.

ISBN                    1-930974-12-4  (paperbound)

Library of Congress Cataloging-in-Publication Data:
Cantwell, Kevin
Something Black in the Green Part of Your Eye/Kevin Cantwell
Library of Congress Catalog Card Number (2001132694)

| | |
|---|---|
| Art Direction | Joseph Wingard |
| Design | Darrin Marvin |
| Production | Paul Sizer |
| | The Design Center, Department of Art |
| | College of Fine Arts |
| | Western Michigan University |
| Printing | Courier Corporation |

# SOMETHING BLACK IN THE GREEN PART OF YOUR EYE

KEVIN CANTWELL

New Issues

WESTERN MICHIGAN UNIVERSITY

*for Betsy*

# Contents

III

## Acknowledgments

I would like to thank the editors of the following magazines for first publishing these poems, most in different versions.

*America:* "Those Days"
*The Bellingham Review:* "That Was the Summer," "Dido's First Theory of the Lyric"
*Commonweal:* "These Heights"
*Gray's Sporting Journal:* "A Recipe for Paper"
*The Journal:* "Advertisement," "Mapping the Savannah River Basin"
*Many Mountains Moving:* "Redwing Blackbird Drawing by a Boy"
*Memphis State Review* (renamed *River City*): "Border States"
*Mississippi Review:* "End of Summer, Below the Fall-line, Central Georgia"
*The New Republic:* "The Darwin Decades," "Marilyn Monroe on a Merry-go-round"
*Nimrod:* "The Pumpkin Fields at Pescadero," "Epistle"
*Paris Review:* "Adam and Eve," "Advent Day at Mumford Quarry Nursery," "The Wooden Trap," "Portrait of Adèle Bloch-Bauer"
*Poetry:* "Sex and Taxes," "Our Plan for Bees"
*Press:* "Acquacotta"
*Quarterly West:* "Holidays"
*River City:* "There's something black in the green part of your eye"
*Shenandoah:* "Color and Chance in the Experimental Garden"
*South Dakota Review:* "Arrows Over the House"
*Southwest Review:* "Learning to Read"
*Tar River Poetry:* "History"
*Western Humanities Review:* "Madonna in Rome," "Dora," "Prisoners Stealing Plums"
*Zone 3:* "Salt"

*"History"* and "Advent Day at Mumford Quarry Nursery" reprinted in the 1995/1996 *Anthology of Magazine Verse & Yearbook of American Poetry,* Monitor Book Company, Palm Springs.

For the gift of time I wish to thank Diane Wood Middlebrook and the Djerassi Resident Artists Program. For support that allowed me to write some of these poems, I thank Macon State College. I would especially like to thank Richard Howard for generously printing so many of these poems. For their friendships, Scott Cairns, Seaborn Jones, Ralph Wilson, and Jeffrey Vasseur. I would also like to thank Frank Bidart, Cam Clay, Larry Levis, Mark Strand, Jacqueline Osherow, and Herb Scott.

To my brother Michael, may you find the living water.

Thou turn'st mine eyes into my very soul,
And there I see such black and grained spots
As will not leave their tinct.

—*Hamlet, III, iv*

I

# Epistle

I promised to write, but as you know
you too have let the years go by.

I *have* heard of course—by the usual
communiqués—that you are dead.

Yet I ask, How dead *is* dead
if I can still see you changing

white tablecloths in the bistro crush?
I wondered if I could joke that day

you called, after I had left town—
but *before* you had passed on—that I

was still alive. You kept asking me,
How *are* you? How *are* you? *O.K.*,

it seemed to me. *O.K.* You listed
the stricken & therefore all of us

who were still alive. I did not ask
after anyone in particular.

We paused, interested in the other
life—but not enough. So you said

that the Eastern Shore had been cold,
but for a night at least a few drinks

at an amber board had kept you there.

## Our Plan for Bees

Clouds tumbling in the wide glass picture window
framed in fruit gilt & the bar mirror in front of us,
   slow, blown breath of the day going by,
horizon of bottles, Scotch & Pernod & high-rise of gin,
   the afternoon a pilsner of summer snow
climbing the updraft between glass buildings,
   small bubbles rising into the underlit, the lowered dark,
dusk the amber pall of whiskeys neat
   & a faint conversation of bees he had heard
I'd found surveying, a storm-broken sycamore & its understory
   vined to thatch, plum & hawthorn & the white tricot
underneath leaves tropic to wind, the trunk
   burned hollow & barrel-chested, columnar
gold stacked in hives where our smoke
   would wend to put them out, bumbling
spill, our talk honey on our tongue if we could take it
   down, one to an axe on either side,
*chink,* bottle-bottom thick, our glasses touch,
   promising we'd do it & night upon us as the last ones
spark from the chimney's rushing heat above us.

## Mapping the Savannah River Basin

Each day, all that summer, I ran the boat,
and eased the throttle wide by increments,
bow cocked against that push to make it go
straight across. We had a boy so afraid
of snakes he would chop them in halves, then fours,
as if each were made for him to learn
his fractions with. We had the sun on us.
If we had to shoot it through a transit,
find it in the metallic glare, it grew
dark, small, like the head of a spike nailed
beyond the boy's boredom. Green sycamores
leaned over the water and were shadows
small in the dull aerial photographs
where we could see, below the surface,
the black hair of weed trailing from jetties
dumped as ballast first. Sometimes out of gas,
the boat would slowly turn, once past a gar, still,
in the current like a thick needle left
in sewing near the window's pouring light.
We would fill the tank in the caesura
roar and think sometimes we heard a person
speak and would turn and question with our eyes
but get the answer waved away by hand,
like mosquitoes brushed from a face, or stars,
the dimples of vertigo—and those looks,
which came to mean we hardly knew each other.
Mainly, it was bank to bank each hundred
yards, fathometer tracing the river
bottom below the molten emerald surge,
which seemed to run at no more speed than glass
rippling. We recalled a crew chief years back:
he had been sent down to the tidal flats

to chain-out and set stone monuments.
He walked them off instead and heaved them past
as far as he would go. What was a foot
out here, or its tenth, under this soupy ebb?
The sandy banks could collapse overnight,
and who but us would know we had been there?
Would it come back to any one of us—
days and now these years gone by us like these
snapping fingers—a burned familiar face
framed like kin in the mirror of the truck
while I backed the trailer down through its S?
Some fool lifting his hand, had we stopped
this time around and bothered to doubt him,
who'd said he'd seen a bright fish fly . . .
yet had begrudged at once the lie of it
when skepticism made us look away or glance
hard at him—we who didn't trust water
to find the sea unless we mapped its way.
Accustomed to such testimony, this time
we waved him off. He'd had his say before
of common birds sprung to fact or second thought,
shedding the jeweled air, the marvelous.

## Choral Lines from the Sumerian

My friend Cassius Clay takes to calling himself Muhammad Ali.

We cut grass on school afternoons.
Then it is summer.

& then it is fall

& the sugarberry trees on both sides of his street go up in yellow,
torches in processional

we can see looking down from his porch roof,
light swelling those leafy wicks.

All night for weeks they drop all day leaves to be raked bright heaps
yard work for the two of us money for grass the smoke we burn
falling from trees.

*In this dark he can see not.*
*Thick was the darkness, light there was none.*

———————

One tends the police radio
in the kitchen, his Scotch, his cup, the bog peat to his lips.

One

lights the paper lantern
of her flesh & stokes the hepatitis
green of her eyes,
drinking herself to death.

Ice trays crack all day in the kitchen
like wet limbs for a fire,

& in Zaire,

Muhammad Ali does his roadwork at dawn,
heat off the road already & off its river of red dust.

*Seven miles he completed, light there was none.*

———————

We drive his old white Continental
far into the county woods, & the open windows
frame quick shots into the trees, the deep aisles

seen once; but we do not see—
we could not *then* see—
my brother, rodman for a land surveyor,
cutting line through his endless night,

the trees cut down in front grown back up behind.

———————

We drive to Cherio for beer & Canadian & ice
& a Styrofoam box we burn
at the end of the rainy weekend,

our fire so large we stand in the cold trees like the dead looking in

& Ali plays possum on the ropes

& at school the next day (as then it is fall),
we slap him on the back,
my friend with the new name of an old boxer:
Mo, the goat-bearded hippie, the Johnny-Winter white
white boy, the flyweight in the crowded hallway

& Ali sits up from the hammock of the ring ropes,
shaking his sleepy head, whispering to Big George
what a bad boy he's been

& stands in the light, his white cat's mouth smiling.

———————

I come to his front door (& then it is winter),
one so drunk she cannot speak,
but I hear him on the balcony roof above,

& I lean back on the porch rail—

this was said of Ali—

as if the roof were on fire & I were leaning backward
out a window looking up.

## Holidays

So-called, these were the feathered spots of primer
left untouched when painting fast and called
to your attention by the foreman
on his rounds your first day at Brown & Williamson.

You had stepped back to admire your brushwork
on the tobacco dryer, which curved away
at the top of its cylinder into the numinous
hue, as above a painted horizon.

You turned from where he'd been to see one spot
you'd missed, then others multiply, suspended,
as you must have seen snow as it first comes down.

———————

Such sloppiness lost you a Saturday since that job
was piecework. And if such calculation made this
kind of sense, it might add to five minutes of roller work;
but on that Saturday you had to move
the ladder by yourself, in a silence so thorough
it was dream's muffled compassion for the sleeping.

———————

The old guys kept gin in the freezer,
the feathered frost intricate on the bottle
as on the windshield of an idling step van,
winter mornings, when the heater softens
two spots like the eyes of a drunk waking up.
They were your future life, in canvas whites
the preparation for a ghostliness
by which they would be made
to bloom, late mornings, in the green shadows of old houses.

---

Those days of drinking when morning came as rain,
when your waking body turned, a garden hose
when loosed water enters it.

You came to think that rain at dawn meant a week of it,
that a day's pay was worth a fly rod, a day off
in the rhododendron hills, late fall,
and a belly stove vented through the van roof
and trailing smoke through an empty campground.

How many nights had the blazing pop of construction scraps
spent itself to the clammy jeans you'd slept in
and cold nails in the ashes?

---

You pick your way around boulders along a mountain creek.
Sometimes on a rise you hear the falls, sometimes
your own breath when you pause. After an hour
you see from a particular angle a glimpse of blue.

Then there it is. Tall, leggy flower sprawled
over a smooth rock like the body of a swimmer
holding a towel to keep the sun from her eyes,
but that color, out of place. Hollyhocks.
How many times had you cut them back
from house foundations to paint the trim?

17

Some pattern in the alluvial sand, herringbone,
from which a single stalk has germinated,
a jacket you pull from where it was jammed.
A garage sale Harris Tweed, yours, lost last summer,
loose in the shoulders, its pockets full of wet sand.

---

You had stood, late winter, in the bay window alcove
of a garden store. You were wasting time.
You had been drinking all morning and now
considered a display of seeds. You thought
you might try a little garden, and you must have
put them in your pocket walking out the door.

## There's something black in the green part of your eye

We were not country people, so John, when he was a boy,
thought one Christmas that we could rent a shotgun just to shoot
   down mistletoe

from the levee sugarberries, rent it for half a day
like anything else we would use once: mandibles of a gear puller,

or a wedding tent's white canvas cloud, through which, like swifts,
tuxed & tailed, black figures disappeared. He said we could stand
   all day

tossing rocks up at the mistletoe, parable of the fools,
I thought, & watch them drop down. As if that's where they came
   from,

he said. Years later, in Montreal, I would see one girl leaning over
another, giving her a *shotgun*. What we called it when we were kids.

Smoke blown through the rolled, reversed tube of a spleef,
red coal inside the shooter's mouth, the passive recipient nodding

Yes. The black hair of the first was thrown forward over the
   other's face.
I remembered someone I had known. We would close our eyes
   that way,

as in kissing. Sometimes they were open & we would make out
the iris's pond-water brown & the green particulate light, flecks

suspended, & our own pupils dark enough to see, tintype
in oval, our own faces in. She said once that she was always
    hungry.

I looked at her, thin under a brother's shirt. She said she didn't know
why she said that. I looked away. She was no one I loved or kissed

enough to think I loved, but someone I drove to the river with,
summer gone & the grass deep in her lungs thick smoke in a
    stream;

& she, her lips this close to mine, would have had enough of it
soon, the corner of a bag & paper without gum twisted to burn

popping along its seedy run, its high, heat, & our rushing blood
like embarrassment coming over us. & once there was no reason
    but happiness,

I suppose, & the gun she had with her from the trunk of her car,
but I let go straight up with a .410 blast & the birds went, in one
    rush, mute,

the two of us stunned, smoke the gray in her green eyes drifting
& then shot like the hard mizzle of sleet falling. Later that day she
    kissed me

between two rooms of her old house. She said, *Don't worry,*
*you won't have to marry me.* We laughed. It was something her
    sister had said

to me once when we were all lit—just when a door left open
slammed shut by a draft, muffled report from inside the house;

that door one of those heart pine slabs that come unhinged,
made that way so a body could go cold & then be carried out.

## Song of the Black Corona

In this bright wind we like to show you
where the dead have stood & long since then where we

have put them down; where one lay down, all
sparks across Hillcrest Avenue, his broken

bike; where one, like a dragged chain, slid his
down Napier; both leaned through the curves; both laid out

a year apart, side by side, beneath
their matching slabs; one with a six-string lead etched

in stone; one, a bass guitar engraved.
"Young" Stribling has his own memorial bridge,

the muddy swirl below; he had gunned
his Indian—coming or going no one

now can say—down Forsyth Road or
up that road; the body of that pugilist,

the Canebrake King, cracked like a dropped egg;
his bridge rumbles all night long beyond the woods.

One, let us show you now, cut in stone,
a ball bat & a glove, hanged himself in jail.

In this bright wind we like to show you
by stepping back from where we stand, *This is where*

*he stood & this is what he said.* One,
on LSD, got lost all night long between

two watersheds; & come next day jumped
two loggers & pounded on their rig; naked

& livid, he whipped at them with snakes;
until a sheriff, then his back-up, & then

the whole day shift of those country boys,
that night, had to take him down, & midnight then

he was the one who hanged himself; &
Michael, first among us born & first to go,

would cut the path himself; would quote, when
he made time come to him, the Gospel of John

where the living water always spills.
We will take you down Walnut Street, bounce along,

across the James Brown, the *I-feel-good*
Bridge; or cross the Redding span; & sometimes

back at night we'll come singing;
sometimes, in the reeds below, just the sleepless

birds. Sometimes this tour means living here;
coffee in hand; a cigarette; a hard clutch

slipping up the hill, the stick someone
riding passenger will have to persuade in-

to gear. We know by heart, in this town,
we know by rote, where the railroad tracks come near

Elizabeth Reed, across the way
from those hippie brothers, side by side. They're down

Rose Hill from where a friend was lowered.
Cranked on speed, he drove a car into the dark

underpass, filmed that month in Huston's
*Wise Blood,* the black blossom where he burned up burned

in concrete, faded by all these years;
but in that sweeping shot of the road from town—

as fresh today as then. Once, we pitched
a yellow tarp in some woods where light has made

houses stand amazed. Downhill—the huge,
watery sun. He & his common law wife-

to-be, back-lit by the early light;
their bodies, stamen & pistil, their limbs, slow

as bees in early frost; my old friend,
black flower now for good, but in that yellow

corolla then (her red wool socks, her
white legs), there were other pleasures of the flesh.

## End of Summer, Below the Fall-line, Central Georgia

Before rain over the old ocean bed poured,
I had read around in it all day,
Milton's great poem, read it like a summer novel,
fat romance that it was. I had forgotten
it late that afternoon, left it on
the wooden bench that swung from a rusty frame
in my parents' yard. When the first white
drops spattered like scuppernong grapes
through the branches of the flowering quince,
I stood to go inside,
and the chair moved faintly,
as if the earth itself still turned on its iron gear.
And pushed ahead of the storm's billowing air,
the rotten smell of the pulp mills,
which I remembered from childhood
as from the chaotic sulfur of place.
And later that evening, I lay in the small bed
I had slept in half my life,
in a room, it seemed, that had not been
touched, as if it were a room on exhibit,
when people did not grow so tall—
shipmaster's cabin with its narrow bunk,
log open to the final entry, still compass.
And yet that tumultuous threat at the sill
was not the ocean's spray flowering
into the baroque, but baby's breath
ecstatic at its bushy crest. And through the drizzle's
lambent screen, the quince glowed,
last color of dusk, as rain over the old ocean
bed poured, last color and pink
as a woman's nipple through a sheer bed-jacket
when she has just come into her milk.
Without let-up, the night grew darker

than even the water sheeting over the eaves,
all of a summer's night, and I slept
deeply, as we sleep as adults
in our parents' homes—and within that shimmering,
familiar volume.

## Border States

We got there casually and soon by drinking to my son,
just born, and now it seems strange, almost wrong

to have kept on shooting down kamikazes
while we tried to remember the border states

of the Civil War, Missouri especially, the paradigm:
the guerrillas of both armies thieving horses,

cooking rye in the steep hills, and wearing the traces,
regimental trousers or a blouse, of two causes.

That was what we were getting at, the edge
or the center failing the union, so much gray,

so much blue, and where they joined to fill out
the dailiness of those years. And if not wrong,

indulgent, for we shaped nothing to celebrate
the new life but the fringe professions of the border states:

thieves at night *shushing* the stone hooves of ponies,
or the pilot guiding his Zero into the burning carrier

to marry what was already dissolving, to become more
or less, in much the same way that shot followed shot

as we ordered and reordered what we wanted
to take us over. We might have welcomed him

with greater formality, the way the midwife had wanted it
when she told me, the *father*, as she said,

to cut him free from his mother, and how I let go
of what I'd already decided, not fighting it, not caring

that someone else's ritual displaced what I wanted—
that *she* do it. Later that evening, drinking

at first to health, I thought that the art was in offering
oneself to the drift until desire or some other attraction

found the shape of things, that old fine music,
which moved the story along, that all things are not

taken or willed, but can be crept up on, white cubes
of sugar in hand, a sweet long story for the large ears

of the fearful, to be coaxed with smooth hands
like any happy soul, untethered from familiar darkness.


*for Ralph Wilson*

## Learning to Read

It is forever and thoroughly wed
to printing our first word
and maybe one letter backward

in a penciled out first name.
And it pleased us! that cozy rote all the same
and the cadenced pull of the King James . . .

And in our little circles we took our turns
to hesitate through dopey Dick and Jane.

Then there was the stage
of jokes only some knew enough to get—

when apples were always more than apples,

when getting it always meant a certain fall
from the literal to the in-between.

It was only a glimmer
through a loose and slightly coarse weave
of something other than our dazzled Eve

robed in the off-color and silhouette,
but we had our laughs and got the antecedent drift,

and back to work we worked the measure of that cursive *it*.

## Arrows Over the House

We sleep like the strewn dead while our son slips out
his bow and his perfect aluminum arrows.

He knows they must sail high to clear
the blistered shingles of the roof, one and

the next launched into the pine and azalea,
where the first is so quickly lost for good

it might be the slate sea that takes it in.
Quickly the other comes to rest mid-flight

in the summer cloud of an evergreen.
At apex it might be used to illustrate

*Foolishness* or that paradox of Zeno.
The shaft reflects the sun so fast at times

it's a filament across the dark but
not there if he tries to look for it again.

He knows this is another sin for which
he can summon no satisfying grief

but promises himself that it's his last
mistake, if chance would drop it down to him,

or if we could wake and clap it down, at will,
like sudden glass, like rain, if he believed

it true enough long enough to believe
it true: our waking motions through the light-

streaked glass; the rain; our clapping hands; distance
that delays the sound; if he could believe it

true, that each day we could open our eyes
and know what it is he thinks we know of him.

## Salt

The untouched beer goes flat. The gold lake of it ripples
when a truck goes past. Instead of chips there's a bowl of salt.

A pinch dropped in boils up a head, and a grain loosens
to fall through the amber column of the draft.

In the handful of times I drank with my father, the two of us alone,
he'd say, "You're getting serious"—when I doubled up beer

with whiskey then went to whiskey by itself. High from the iron nest
of a building going up, acetylene drips straight down.

Through the reversed blue enamel letters of the window,
I watch a dog who doesn't know his Homer bum scraps in
    falling rain.

There was a time when standing he excused himself, in the thick
formality of such unsteadiness, his face drawn down

the long bar mirror, disappearing, until he was a rustle of clothing
when he returned, slower it seemed, to whom this could be said:

*Brush the crumbs from your dark suit. Bootblack your coffin hair.*

*for my father*

## These Heights

On Everest, beneath my blanket tent,
I shook my Ray-O-Vac if it went out,
    palmed the lens when I heard my parents shout
upstairs, again, *Lights out!* Then from a vent,
    cigarette smoke and their low talk's ascent
through heating duct, murmurous as my doubt
        that a radio's call, now fading out,
        could reach that col where their bottled air was spent.

These days, my mother trails a plastic hose
        to breathe in emphysema's altitudes.
She's learned to flip it like a climber's rope,
        and, by one, mount the stairs, rest, as if snows
fell around her, and, in slow lassitude,
        dulled the glittering rise of what she hopes.


*for my mother*

## Those Days

What was it yesterday—that other day—
but a smeared background mired in smoke,
            and a whispered *hush* before the Mass
was said, car doors closing outside in heavy rain,
      that steady pouring, and bumping clouds,
hesitant, like furniture moved upstairs; and by a half-inch
      brush, the unsteady horizon in gray oil applied?
            What holy day was that, feast or privation?
The snap of fingers got my attention.
            Had I been dreaming. Homily or sleep.
My mother. Light pouring through
      the vinegar-clean glass, and the of-this-earth
*shoulds* of whatever day it was.
            Creak of oven door. Some days a kiss.

## Advent Day at Mumford Quarry Nursery

These flagstones stagger as discarded graves
on which engravers botched a line or date,
or split the granite's flaw; a stream-cut groove's
water slows; headstones prop an iron grate
through which the azure pool drains inhuman
cold; but green of mistletoe and holly
wreaths sell briskly, sold by the home for men,
who seem unmindful of the pitched, hilly
walks; speechless, they seem yet unamazed
and fetch poinsettia by the armful,
or mulch, for those who look beyond the fall
come to solstice dark and these fallow days.
Alms or extravagance of *crème de menthe*—
we write it off to get us by lean months.

## Redwing Blackbird Drawing by a Boy

Thick as halo-leaf around the listless heads of saints, this gold
sun in the upper corner is a convention but wrong. You are
beginning to draw things the way things are, green crayon
through a*qua*, which means, you tell me, *water.*

You want to be good. You loved your teachers once, but less and
less now that you begin to love yourself, yet offering one
goldenrod from a ditch and, speckled like the chest of a brown
thrasher, an apple. *It's for you*, you say,

you who catches her by the wrist only to give her a harmless
account of a cat in the Ovidian dusk: finch alive in its full black
cheeks, whiskers stiff and two yellow wings. *What strange gills!*
you whisper, nearly frightening her.

Today, you would have looked up from your long division, bird
sound piercing the hush, to draw this spoon-billed anomaly
from nothing but that sound and the lack of a #1 brush. The sea
grass bends. The wind is just right: the nest,

round like a cup, tips to mean *tribulation*, the eggs nearly liquid,
drops in the tributary ocean and a single colored egg at the lip
almost joining (the Eighteenth Century might say) the Tribe of
Fish. Lank hair cowling your forgetfulness,

your muttering privacies, you will find a hound to be bottle-fed,
brought back from worms and ticks bloating from its mange like
hot-air balloons over a summer commons. You will break last
year's marigolds, press their seeds into your pant cuffs,

a game for your little bird, for whose broken wing you made a
cast from an envelope corner and how it will come so suddenly:
your nights patient as a child's grief, a leaking roof to map in
the plaster ceiling the continent of those months in a first
    apartment—

the morning mirror and the Goth mask of your insomnia.


*for John*

**II**

# This Talk of Marlowe at Deptford

In an hour it will be June, but for now
some commotion in the back rises but moves on
after a crash like a *Sportster* knocked down.
There's a rush for the door then nothing but an owl

startled from the white-washed stand of beech trees
in the yard crossed by shadows of the branches' sway.
From four hundred years ago—words, hearsay,
whispers from the drabbing stalls; but now we see these

wits & college boys jot from the Inquest
of the Coroner this bar napkin doggerel:
*One Robert Poley his mouth his nostrils*
*stopped with dirt. One Nicholas Skeres his eyes once wet*

*with happiness, & said Ingram Frizer*
*he knifes poor Kit who's hurt* . . . Christopher Marlowe stabbed
through the eye; but in this bar a just-stubbed
cigarette sends up its smoke like a rope riser

without which, when pulled up, we cannot go
to Heaven. What draws us here is the quick needle
that stitched the living to the dead. The dill
his killers crushed with careless feet those years ago

on their afternoon walk sends us the rank
brine from the pickle jar on the barmaid's fingers.
She waits while these three frats slowly figure
their bill for darts & pretzels & what they drank

to get them ready for tomorrow's test.
Outside, like slick starlings polished as they steer,
a crowd of Harleys rides away—to stares
both expectant & bored—to play up & so twist

crystal meth, fronted by a go-between,
into a debt called in abruptly, like blank verse
enjambed & razored off. Now the silvers
of black bikes grow smaller until they can't be seen;

& Marlowe, from a camp account, will stand
& try to brush it off, like wood chipped by a sledge
(tapped until a tree leans from a pushed-in wedge)
or the fine dust of light the dead clap from their hands.

## The Wooden Trap

The held cry of a hawk makes Thomas Hardy think
to make her believe it's a newborn's cry she hears.
Milk wets through her blouse. The other women know
at once. That's chapter one. How it starts
to grow while above his head the cumuli
accumulate. The August fields waver beyond
the privet hedge. He's given up the novel
for poetry. The women look at each other.
One counts out change on a plank counter.
That's that she says. Then exposition's drift
to flashback: how a horseshoe loosens;
how when leading the horse the master returns.
Not angry, only to get it done right.
How she presses under the eaves of the shed
with him while the afternoon rain comes down
so hard they are nearly soaked anyway.
The editorial omniscient bites his tongue.
Innocent as it goes. The scent of windfall
rises up through the apple tree from the ground.
Some of the leaves bronze even now. There's no
turning back but that's getting ahead of ourselves.
There's Hardy. Shoes a disgrace. Canvas gaiters
undone and one foot on top of the ladder
where it narrows at the highest rung, the worn wood
twice the width of a stirrup, and one foot
in the crotch of a limb. He has it all
worked out. She's in another country where rumor's made
a place for her. *Where's the little one?*
they ask, but she presses past them into the lane.
It serves her right but no one says it
so that she hears. A limb tumbles through the green
cloud of foliage. And then another. He cuts it back

to make it bear, though a neighbor's stopped to tell him
it's ill-advised so late in the season.
She finds a place for herself as a domestic
until the governor says a girl's come back.
They'll have to let her go. It's dusk. The clouds
go pink to shell. He folds the little saw.
The ladder widens to its base. A trick of perspective
also that lures the gopher into the wooden box
he's set in its tunnel, the hole which looks
like an exit, the end of the tunnel, daylight,
but smaller than its head and those footsteps
on the earth above, which pause and anticipate
her every turn, and block her escape
with a garden fork plunged into the lyric dark.

## The Darwin Decades

They knew so much of what they could know
in caricature. A dozen Amelias
dwindled beneath the blush
peignoirs of popular prose—
and the great gardens of the empire
filled out to shade
the public lawns. And in private studies
and paintings, the milky tonnage
of ice loomed through the green-
gray oils and the sure laws of motion.
Those were the periodic elements.
From journal cartoon to opinion page
that inked ape coming of age—
becoming what he was, only a man
pinned against a secular evidence.

And what could be slowed by only a million
words. Thousands of children
*(For thame nevir mair wul I see)* never
claiming the tactile dazzle of the material
life. And letters without number
stretched thin across a private means,
and each began *My dearest one* . . .
There were more, and so many
famished behind the architecture of steam-
driven looms, ten thousand children nearly ten
reciting *Edward*
and biding their own anonymous time.

## Color and Chance in the Experimental Garden

1

Near where some weeks before the monk Mendel
had heaped and doused
the uprooted pyracanthas with coal oil
and set them blazing
to smoke into smoke rags
scoring the blue corridors of white,

the girl walks the Vienna road
while he pauses from planting
the cleared garden with two thousand pea plants
while he watches her
color when he does not look away.

All the blossoms that first summer were white.

2

He pencils in ledgers and a journal
what changes he can see: the tallied drift
gathering momentum: the tall pea plants
crossed by manual pollination
into the short pea plants—and his students' failing marks
passing into his white hair

3

and Bismarck's horses emphatic in the long mud of Europe.

4

Sweet spring yellow summer
purple where autumn's burning glass,
the lenticular sky,
welters at its bevel toward December.
He lets the garden lapse
when he can use no more numbers,
and so the birds pass

every kind of seed into the careful rows.

5

The evening before Mendel presents his paper
to the society he retraces whole sections
of Darwin and then the entire book
of Genesis. Seven days,
perhaps, he says to himself, knowing
the idea is not new,
but a picture almost emerges
of a great rainy blast
followed by a million years of tall grasses . . .

His audience shivers in the chilly lecture hall,
and some doze by the stove.
Others put their pencils to work.

6

In the last year of his life,
he forgets prayer, thinks about momentum
and acceleration. Cholera sweetens
the air when the school board makes him an administrator.
And the finches nest where the trellises

slump into the garden paths
where they winter

and fall. He reads nothing
but the first lines
of John and the entire Genesis,
fattens on chocolate and Burgundy.

7

On an evening in early July he sits on a stone
bench smoking a cigar
and watches a boy ride a bicycle
so slowly he might never
reach the porch of a young woman before dark.

He thinks about offspring, color
and characteristics as he walks the loamy path
around the garden. He sees a pink blossom.

Curious and nearing the tangle of peas,
he understands. Two pure colors
next to each other. They drift
together again as he backs away.

*Insinuate.* He keeps looking up
that word. In the dusking hues, that dot
goes lavender, like an exotic moth fluttering
that girl's pale dress

white to lavender to pink to purple until color itself
hesitates.

*for Betsy*

## Prisoners Stealing Plums

*How* do they think they got here in the first place?
But that's harsh. They think what we have all thought.
That no one will see them. That it would be a sin
to let this go to waste, spoil, or watch the birds
go at them, or these kids, let them have them
who would fling them as stones at their friends
now who wish that school would let them go for the year,
who know that their small crimes will be
brushed off. An eye put out? They have one more. You see
it's all a joke—to those too who have not lost their nerve
in the dark grove, who take brief leave
from the high rick where they will hang
their drop cloth, where one has shrugged
his robe to stand and sing, unnoticed.

## History

*is what hurts,* someone has said,
and what you must repeat
if you fail that class the first time,

taking it again with others, like you,
who show up, pie-faced
and unafraid, because the worst has happened
already, that summer is spent

sitting behind a girl
whose shoulders would darken
as the weeks go by,
so that you mistake for a pink strap
the unburned skin of her back,

as if you saw her shoulders while she bathed,
as she raised two hands
of water to her face,
and then asked for you
to hand her a towel,

she, whose back freckles with August,
as would a russet apple,
muscling its place among the leaves.

## Adam and Eve

And now they have already begun to go,
in Albrecht Dürer's piece, a little soft
    around the waist; she has, at least; and slow
to leave, they must, as sand begins to sift
    inexorably through its narrow waist of glass.
Her flesh grown thick we take to be a son.
    Those awful woods, untouched by ray of sun,
go still; hence this study and his early gloss
    of *Melancholia*; hence her touching smile,
which never fades completely, nor the leaves,
    which stay, and free their hands for the small
tasks at which they've grown so clumsy: the loaves
    which sour by that cause: that which so divides,
    yet which of pleasure is not so devoid.

*He will show you a large room upstairs, set out in readiness . . .*

Mark 14:15

When I asked my class to Lee & Eddie's,
   some dropped their eyes, & one made this odd show
of looking sideways, but all let me know
   by a show of hands that they would meet me,
Thursday, at what they'd *heard* as Leonetti's—
   where bread would be set out by the slow
waiter & wine poured until each would grow
   despondent when the wine would empty.
But here were ribs & slaw, not Italian!
   A pig on a sign with a bouquet of collards
told them this! The waitress named Carmine
   *told* them this! There *were* no vegetarian
plates, she said—except for the greens & lard—
   then poured their spilling waters to the brim.

## Madonna in Rome

Such daily titter from the Vatican!
Provisionals! One editorial
    would say that she could never be more real
than the wish that wind, like the Rubicon,
    be caught by net; and so I too wished
a miracle: a pair of tickets, One!
            were it such that joy be that hard won.
Outside her hotel we stood, the unwashed
    drizzle undershot by television
lights, under which we too were struck at rest-
            less wait, but then, O, my skin felt like dust
touching it. *Comuna vérgine!*
    a man had called. She stood as if to rule—
        in her *bathrobe!*—at the concrete rail.

## Dora

She had paused, mid-sentence . . .
I must have been distracted, too.
Narcotic dusk of barn swallows and summer's calendar
dark on its page—that, and the tobacco scent
swept between us down the stairs. She said, *I can't
remember.* Then there was a quiet snap.
I saw she had a little purse, fastened at her waist—
maroon and velvet petals sewn in suede,
its clasp, two herons in a silver twist.
Her unconscious fingers toyed inside,
worried what it was that would set her off,
her slip's white hem where the surf would fold the sea
(*Speak!* I had wanted to say, but blushed)
back, yet roar in a pink conch I had held.

# Portrait of Adèle Bloch-Bauer

*after Klimt*

All this gold and silver for her to have
a sitter's fifty-minute hour go on
  past lunch. Stomach mewing. Saffron shafts
pouring their pooling heats of midday sun.
  Eyes all over her & feline & blond
deltas on the kohl kimono she wears
  as if she were not brunette and all his
purring cats rubbing to try her dark mood.
  She smells that lunch is made, tomatoes,
sliced thin as the red fabric he had tried
  to eat off her nipples, & cucumber
scent drawn through the house by a closing door.
  Her mouth waters. She's wet where he touches
the paint. She smells the oil. She tastes the salt.

  She peels the cucumber, her breath leaden.
She knows they will not come where she works.
  A kitchen girl. Making lunch for those two.
Pumpernickel toast. Salt. Pepper. Olive
  oil. She smells the paint from the studio
when she stands at the door to listen.
  She sits in the chair, puts her feet up
on the table, unbuttons beneath her
  dress. Dares them to find her like this. Open
where she can have it inside, oiled, lucent,
  her head put back, her red mouth, her almond
lids. She hears someone laugh when she's finished
  & slices it thin for an appetizer
  & salts and oils it before she slips out.

## Marilyn Monroe on a Merry-go-round

*photograph by Eve Arnold, 1954*

She's turned a page in Joyce and goes around
so slowly we can't see it turn; and still
    the trees above the summer grass surround
the summer star, who on that catherine wheel
    forgets herself—and Eve, who's framed this shot
and once held on herself beyond her will:
    her legs, her arms to stone, the sun, this dot
of ink. It's Molly Bloom who asks to feel
    her *breasts all perfume yes* . . . or it's a pose
that we might see such concentration dry
    her lips. By those few pages left suppose
we know the passage, which runs breathlessly
    toward each susurrus of a quickened wish;
    suppose the stars, pinwheels, another *yes* . . .

# Acquacotta

*[Toasts] come to us from the English, who . . . put a piece of toast on the bottom of a beer pot. Whoever drank last got the toast. One day Anne Boleyn, then the most beautiful woman in England, was taking her bath, surrounded by the lords of her suite. [E]ach took a glass, dipped it in the tub, and drank to her health. All but one . . . [who] said, I am waiting for the toast.*
—Alexandre Dumas

> First, bring a pony's weight of water,
> unadulterated, to a boil.
> Let stand until its one last bubble
> rises like a diver's face ballooned
>     and bright from a minute's lack of air.
> Have Anne Boleyn step in, but careful,
>     lest she die young. Some will want the Queen
> post coital, lending, you will have guessed,
>     the ocean's undertow as its salt.
> Crush some salvia between your hands.
>     Rinse with warm olive oil. Dip in bath.
> Let mull. At one hour, add whole scallions,
>     or substitute the few days she's had
> without a bath. You must not leave her
>     alone, since solitude has made her
> weep in the past, which will add more salt
>     when cooks today call for less of it.
> Read to her, while the stock reduces,
>     a letter that's made her body flush,
> yet closes with this: *I have waited
>     too long to send this. We are released.*
> *We are released.* Do not let her weep,
>     but dilute the broth with some water
> shaken from rinsed, bunched oregano
>     if she does. Ladle out on the heels
> of week-old bread. Travelers call this
>     *cooked water.* She must bear the King's son
> to live. Avert your eyes when she stands,
>     lest she place your hand where the child swells.

61

## Dido's First Theory of the Lyric

It is true that once she too had fallen asleep to the unpunctuated
cant of some stranger's account; he, a clerk, reporting

only what had come down to him by whisper; that on a found
island—
a fetish sect: women who believed that all must go back

to where they lost their minds with grief; there begin anew;
he, a clerk explaining that pause & form & flagging lull, while she

drifted off; had a dream of dropping off, between dream's swift nod
& a harsh, sudden laugh in the herb garden dusk; causing her
davening

drowse to cease; & then months later, the stranger arrives at the
docks;
his skin, not touching yet; hers, the desire; his, the touch; rain,

the rain beating leaves to shreds outside their hidden cave; he,
summoned too soon by the goddess's whisper; she, let down,
over her

combs, over her anointing oils; & hers, the pause beyond that
emptying; her chilled skin flushed before the blood's drain; her hair

rent & her flesh mooned up beneath her fingernails & all the wind-
shorn candles blown out by a drape ripped open; she, a droop wet

with night on the patio; the date palm's patois rustling: the luff
of the clerk's murmur; hers, the sea; the sea, before her; she,

asking that madness cease; she, saying, if you go do not speak; she,
from sleep: let me help you with the fire; here is my body, my voice,

the oil; here is my body, my body, the wick; if you go why won't you
speak? That thirst; that surf; hers, the voice ripped out of the sea;

hers, the servant girl pouring water into a plum-black bowl, the girl
not knowing what to do; she, the Queen; hers, the porcelain sky

& the boiling pour splitting the ceramic, rim to basin; the painted
gull split from the painted cloud; the cracking tear: the lightning

lit-up sea.

## The Pumpkin Fields at Pescadero

    Jays on the glass wind, crows
from the blue tree line. It's September.
    There's no hurry to die. I call you
from a grocery store pay phone
    & watch two field workers eat
two green coconut Snoballs.
    You are three thousand miles away.
The stems are being cut, the pumpkins
    stacked as *calabazas*, stones.
Frost, sun, the weathering slow years
    of a week. We will look like that
one day, our faces toothless in the light,
    heads so weightless that the filament heat
will rise through holes we've carved for ears.
    The far-off Pacific lifts, glints.
Your voice is tired. Home in a week,
    I ask if it has rained, if our son
is sad at night. One of the workers
    has feathers in his shirt pocket—
hummingbirds: costas, black-chinned,
    or blue-throated, thus quivered to be graced
by love I am told. You tell me
    how happy I sound. You tell me
that the white star of a late gardenia
    made you stand, puzzled, at the dark window.
I tell you that I hear owls
    in the madrone trees at night
& coyotes practicing their human griefs.
    I am sorry. I planted the trees
at home for you, the maple, to shade
    the porch, the elbertas at the lip

of the drop, the line of myrtle;
    & the shrubs, forsythia & the Russian sage;
heather, lilies, Japonica, & a fig
    I turned in its pot all summer
as once you had turned in a dress
    I had given you, before a mirror, wondering
if the leaf-print was for you.
    Our words are hands submerged
where broken glass carves its iceberg
    in the warm soap of dishwater.
After a while we hang up. The two men have gone
    back to the field. My white shirt loose,
the vines loop my feet in that field,
    pants plastered in mud, my moon blade,
my worn knife in hand. I will carve,
    seed & pulp scooped out, this pumpkin
shell masked by thumbed-on ochre.
    I will wear it in the sun until the jays
strip me of my eyes & a hummingbird
    nests in the pocket of my shirt.

## That Was the Summer

It would not rain & the ditches dried up
into the cross-hatched cracks of glazed mud;
    months; months; but one night the Old Testament
        torrentials,
afterword, I like to think, of the Wicked Book,
    the Bible hand-set in the *Incunabula* by a printer
who left out *Not* in the commandment against Wishing.
    You can keep one, it is said, but not both, either a wife,
or a peach grove. The work is long; sleep, never enough when
        it's cold
    in spring; or the cold itself, never the hours you need of it.
The trees get sprayed with nozzled mist to insulate the buds
    with coated ice & the cold, the dark, will light the reds,
the blues, the burning stars & the old nurserymen will say
    you must whip them to make them come
to fruit. That summer, the dwarf elberta, the only tree to escape
    a freeze, bore a handful. I held each to my face, cradled
like the last gold ornament lifted down.
    *Cherish in hand.* I'd planned to pick them after work
but found them gone the next day. My neighbor
    came to mind & then the gardener I remembered
as leaves blown in the insect machinery of his work.
    I thought of his wife having them fed to her,
each touching her plum lips & now I believe
    that none of this is true, but that the daylight rats
from the trees came down in brazen purpose,
    or those at night, in the pomade of sewer slick,
& clambered up the tree in starless quiet & feasted
    in the dark, as we will do, at such ease
we believe we have been forgiven.

## A Recipe for Paper

A thread-tied snip of John's first haircut—
when I still fished with flies, thinking
    I'd slow a German brown enough to lift it
through the pewter skin of the light above
    & learned what anyone could see in the open
register of Izaak Walton about what floats
    & how soon a cold stream bedraggles whim.
I found some crack-willow instead & peeled
    a desultory whip to flay the blowsy webs,
trying to remember while breaking weeds
    the way I'd come & later I cooked rose-hip tea
along the feldspar run where the mica tricks itself
    into believing more of itself than even the stars
outflung, my little stove roaring up the burnished flue
    some call the interstices; & smoking
last summer's cigarette left in a flybox
    I bumped the white-gas Whisperlite to an extra burn.
I made confetti of my ballpoint map of these
    three *cricks* my Michigan cousins call them
still, the paper pieces tumbling in the boiling roll
    & lift of updraft's ashen rise & the pulp
soaked in the cold overnight tea & cut onion skin
    & the crack-willow flaxed by pounding it
to a screen laid flat on a rock to catch the paper slopped
    from a coffee can, which drums when filled,
& then your dream of what you asked of me
    inside you from behind, incising with a red Bic
these little marks on your back, a passage from the late Colette
    & then starlight's watermark, your sleeping face.

## Sex and Taxes

Plum black & the blush white of an apple
shoulder, melon & cream, in tones to list
    the flesh; in light, washed colors off at last
& textures sheer with damp I slowly pull
    from you with your quick help. Weekend's ample
procrastinations to forget the least
    of what we want to do. April, half a blast
of cold, half new light, green & simple.
    Now dusk. Now fear. We pencil what we owe
on this short form, our numbers good enough.
    The goose-neck glare undoes how we spent the day.
Each bite each bee-sting kiss each bitten O
    all aftertaste. Later, at the drop-off,
postmark queue, we joke: *Now we can die!*

# Advertisement

*What a deale of cold business doth a man mis-spend the better part of a life in!*
*scattering complements, tendring visits, gathering and venting news, following*
*Feasts & Plays, making a little winter-love in a darke corner.*
—Ben Jonson, Discoveries

You may not live in this city anymore, but you visited my apartment with my wife's friend. You may not remember, but you read a Louise Bogan poem to me. Well, you looked at me when you finished. We lived in our first apartment above Highland Avenue—my wife & I. The walls were of the faintest lavender. We had just been married. We had a Japanese black pine on our black iron landing. We had a painting with a little dog on a rug. We had in our kitchen our dog on a little rug. We moved soon after to a city where it snowed when I ran late at night. I did not think of you. We moved, again, back to this state. We lived on a pond. A blue heron worked the edge of the water, like the needle of an old Singer machine stitching down so quickly, then pausing. You had *The Blue Estuaries*, the gutter & glue, the threads strained, turned back. That concerned me while you read. I thought the book was mine, but as it turned out it was yours. Mine was on the shelf behind you where you sat on your heels. You can understand my confusion. The three of you were so beautiful that afternoon. The windows were open. Maples pressed against the screens. You wore a blue skirt & gold sandals. Our red dog walked into the room to step on our feet. My wife had cut some flowers from the field that day. They were in a glass vase, a wedding gift. If you read this tell Robin to take a day, come down & visit Betsy. Tell her that she is loved & that they can sit down by the peach trees & drink red wine. They can even smoke cigarettes. They can sun their bare legs. Tell her that the mosquitoes are slow this year. Tell her that they can talk in peace. Tell her that I will cut some pears for them & that I will cook a summer omelet with yellow squash. I will wake them when it is ready. You must have a family yourself, children who come to you with sleepy faces in the morning. Tell Robin that before she drives the long drive home that we will light candles on the thwarts of the black canoe & push it across the water into the dusk.

# Notes

1) The title of the book is a line of dialogue from Roman Polanski's *Chinatown* (Paramount, 1974); 2) Epigraph, III, iv, 405 *Hamlet*; 3) "Choral Lines from the Sumerian": Lines of refrain from Tablet IX, *Gilgamesh*, trans., William Ellery Leonard (Viking, 1934); in the documentary about the 1974 Foreman-Ali fight in Kinshasa, Zaire, *When We Were Kings* (1996, directed by Leon Gast), George Plimpton describes Ali in his *rope-a-dope* defense as a man leaning out a window backward to see what was on his roof; 4) "Song of the Black Corona": Two motorcyclists/musicians are Duane Allman and Berry Oakley, members of the Allman Brothers Band; their song "In Memory of Elizabeth Reed" comes from a headstone in Rose Hill Cemetery, Macon, GA; W. L. "Young" Stribling, Jr., lost the heavyweight bout to Max Schmelling in 1931; Otis Redding; 5) "This Talk of Marlowe at Deptford": prompted by *The Reckoning: The Murder of Christopher Marlowe*, by Charles Nicholl (University of Chicago Press, 1992); a *Sportster* is a bike model made by Harley-Davidson; 6) "*History*": Title and part of the first line (*is what hurts . . .*) from *The Political Unconscious* (Cornell University Press, 1981), by Frederic Jameson; 7) "*He will show you a large room upstairs, set out in readiness . . .*": (Mark 14:15), *The New English Bible with the Apocrypha* (The Oxford University Press, 1971); 8) "Madonna in Rome": Italics translate the title of her album and her song *Like a Virgin* (Warner Brothers, 1984); opening simile prefigured by Wyatt's famous poem; 9) "Dora": Speculates on Freud's well-known case history; 10) "Marilyn Monroe on a Merry-go-round": Italics from the last page of *Ulysses*, by James Joyce (Vintage, 1961); 11) "That Was the Summer": Italics from *The Poetry of Robert Frost* (Holt, Rhinehart, and Winston, 1969); 12) "Acquacotta": Epigraph from *Dictionary of Cuisine: A Literary & Practical Guide to the Pleasures of the Table*, by Alexandre Dumas, Edited, Abridged and Translated by Louis Colman (Fireside: Simon and Schuster, 1990); 13) "Advertisement": Epigraph from *Discoveries* addendum to *Ben Jonson: The Complete Poems* (Yale University Press, 1975).

photo by Betsy Lerner

Kevin Cantwell lives with his wife and son in Georgia, where he teaches literature and writing at Macon State College. Among other awards, he has won the *River City* award and an Academy of American Poets Prize. His poems have appeared in many magazines, including *Paris Review*, *Poetry*, and *The New Republic*.

## New Issues Poetry & Prose

Editor, Herbert Scott

James Armstrong, *Monument In A Summer Hat*
Michael Burkard, *Pennsylvania Collection Agency*
Anthony Butts, *Fifth Season*
Kevin Cantwell, *Something Black in the Green Part of Your Eye*
Gladys Cardiff, *A Bare Unpainted Table*
Kevin Clark, *In the Evening of No Warning*
Jim Daniels, *Night with Drive-By Shooting Stars*
Joseph Featherstone, *Brace's Cove*
Lisa Fishman, *The Deep Heart's Core Is a Suitcase*
Robert Grunst, *The Smallest Bird in North America*
Mark Halperin, *Time as Distance*
Myronn Hardy, *Approaching the Center*
Edward Haworth Hoeppner, *Rain Through High Windows*
Cynthia Hogue, *Flux*
Janet Kauffman, *Rot* (fiction)
Josie Kearns, *New Numbers*
Maurice Kilwein Guevara, *Autobiography of So-and-so: Poems in Prose*
Ruth Ellen Kocher, *When the Moon Knows You're Wandering*
Steve Langan, *Freezing*
Lance Larsen, *Erasable Walls*
David Dodd Lee, *Downsides of Fish Culture*
Deanne Lundin, *The Ginseng Hunter's Notebook*
Joy Manesiotis, *They Sing to Her Bones*
Sarah Mangold, *Household Mechanics*
David Marlatt, *A Hog Slaughtering Woman*
Paula McLain, *Less of Her*
Sarah Messer, *Bandit Letters*
Malena Mörling, *Ocean Avenue*
Julie Moulds, *The Woman with a Cubed Head*
Marsha de la O, *Black Hope*
C. Mikal Oness, *Water Becomes Bone*
Elizabeth Powell, *The Republic of Self*
Margaret Rabb, *Granite Dives*
Rebecca Reynolds, *Daughter of the Hangnail*
Martha Rhodes, *Perfect Disappearance*
Beth Roberts, *Brief Moral History in Blue*